I0086938

Copyright © 2013 by Sensitive Solutions
All rights reserved
No part of this book may be used or reproduced in any manner
whatsoever without the written permission of the publisher.
Printed in the United States
ISBN: 0985125616
ISBN-13: 978-0985125615

# Rest your Rattle

by Lexi Parker

Illustrations by Rose Bennington

*For the families I've been lucky enough to work with.*

*Your effort, resilience, and love inspire me everyday.*

More of your favorite characters from this series of books

**Bob**

**Petey**

**Lana**

Ralphie Rattles lived in Dunesville Desert.
He shared a dried up den with Grandpa Rattles.

Ralphie was a riot.  He had the best jokes in all of Dunesville!
But there was just one problem… When Ralphie got upset he would
cause a ruckus. This meant that he would get so upset that he didn't
know how to calm back down.

He caused a ruckus when no one else wanted to play rock, rattle, and roll.

He caused a ruckus if he lost the tongue drop race.

But he especially would cause a ruckus if no one laughed at his joke.
One day he was telling a joke to Rosie Rattles, "What do you call a snake
without clothes on? Snake-Ed," Rosie Rattles didn't get it and she didn't laugh.

Ralphie got upset that Rosie Rattles didn't get his joke. His scales turned red and his rattle started to shake. **RATTLE RATTLE BANG BANG.** Rosie Rattles slithered away as fast as she could.

When he realized that he had caused a ruckus Ralphie started to cry. Grandpa Rattles slithered over. "What's the matter Ralphie?"
"I caused a ruckus and now Rosie Rattles doesn't want to play with me."

Grandpa slithered closer.
"It's alright Ralphie, you just need to learn some magic tricks
to rest your rattle." "Really?" Ralphie perked up.

"Of course! Try the trick Freeze and Breathe. As soon as you feel your rattle star to rumble, freeze, take a deep breath through your nose, and let it out of your mouth. Just like blowing out birthday candles. Try it." Ralphie tried it.

"Good! Alright, let's go to the den and try the Disappearing Act. If your rattle won't rest, slither to a safe spot as fast as you can and let your rattle ruckus. Once you rest your rattle you can come back out and play."

"Watch, I'll show you."
Grandpa Rattles slithered away to **RATTLE RATTLE BANG BANG.**
Ralphie watched in amazement.

'I know,' thought Grandpa. 'I'll give Ralphie some practice.'
"Why don't you tell me one of those jokes of yours Ralphie?"
"Sure! What's a snake's favorite subject?…Hissstory."

Ralphie looked up ready for Grandpa to be cracking up, but he wasn't!
"I don't get it," Grandpa pretended. Ralphie started to feel his scales
turn red and his rattle stated to rumble.

"Quick," Grandpa yelled, "try your magic tricks."
Ralphie tried Freeze and Breathe, but his rattle was still rumbling.
He thought fast and slithered off to do the Disappearing Act…

RATTLE RATTLE BANG BANG.

Once his rattle had rested Ralphie slid out with a frown on his face.
"What's wrong?" asked Grandpa. "I caused a ruckus," Ralphie mumbled.
"You did the Disappearing Act and I'm so proud of you for that!"
Grandpa exclaimed. "Just keep practicing and you'll be able to rest
your rattle in no time."

The next day Ralphie slithered off to find Rosie Rattles. "Rosie, I'm sorry for causing a ruckus, but can I try to tell you that joke again?"
Rosie was a little nervous, but agreed. "What do you call a snake without clothes on? Snake-Ed!" Rosie Rattles still didn't get it.

Ralphie started to feel his scales turn red and his rattle rumble. 'Quick,' he thought 'Freeze and Breathe.' Ralphie closed his eyes and blew out imaginary birthday candles.  After the third breath, his rattle was resting on the floor.

"Snake-Ed rhymes with naked," Ralphie calmly explained. "Oh, I get it!"
Rosie Rattles rolled on the floor, hissing with laughter. "Ralphie, you're a riot!
Let's go tell the other rattles your joke!"

And off they slithered into the dessert to find all their rattle friends.

**THE END**

www.ingramcontent.com/pod-product-compliance
Lightning Source LLC
Chambersburg PA
CBHW041242040426
42445CB00004B/121